MERRILL READING PROGRAM

CATCH ON

Based on the philosophy of Charles C. Fries

Authors

Phyllis Bertin
Educational Coordinator
Windward School
White Plains, New York

Eileen Perlman
Learning Disabilities Specialist
White Plains Public Schools
White Plains, New York

Dr. Cecil D. Mercer
Professor of Education
University of Florida
Gainesville, Florida

Mildred K. Rudolph

Rosemary G. Wilson

 **SRA McGraw-Hill**

Columbus, Ohio

A Division of The McGraw·Hill Companies

TABLE OF CONTENTS

SRA/McGraw-Hill

A Division of The McGraw·Hill Companies

Copyright © 1999 by SRA/McGraw-Hill. All rights reserved.
Except as permitted under the United States Copyright Act, no
part of this publication may be reproduced or distributed in
any form or by any means, or stored in a database or retrieval
system, without prior written permission from the publisher.

Printed in the United States of America.

Send all inquiries to:
SRA/McGraw-Hill
8787 Orion Place
Columbus, Ohio 43240-4027

ISBN 0-02-674708-1

2 3 4 5 6 7 8 9 BCH 02 01 00

pot	pots
cot	cots
lot	lots
Dot	dots
hot	

mom

cat	hat	pat	pot
cot	hit	pit	not
got	hot	pot	lot

Dot

Dot is Dan and Jan's mom.
Dot said, "I have to have a lot
of suds for the van.
I got dots of mud on it.

Dot got lots of suds for the van.

She got rid of the mud
with lots of hot suds.

Dan's Mix

Dan ran up to his mom.
"Mom," he said, "I have a mix
for hot buns.
If Jan can cook ham in a pot,
I can fix hot ham on hot buns."

"Fix the mix for the buns,"
said Mom.

"The ham is hot," said Jan.
"Fix lots of buns for Dad, Mom,
and me."

Dot's Nap

Dot took a nap on a cot in the van.

She got up and said, "The van is hot.

I cannot nap on cots."

Jan ran up to her mom.

"Mom," she said, "Dan has a lot of hot buns for us."

Mom said, "And I can cook lots of hot ham.

Dan and Dad can have it on buns.

But I am hot.

I cannot have hot ham and buns."

hop	hops
mop	mops
pop	pops
top	tops

box

fox

hit	tap	map	fix
hip	tip	mop	fox
hop	top	pop	box

A Top for Pam

Dot has a box for little Pam.
In the box are tops.

Pam looks into the box
and sees the tops.
She taps a top.
It pops up!
She taps it and taps it.
Pam hops to Dot with the tops.
"Tops are fun," said Pam.

Dot hugs her.
"Little Pam is fun for me,"
said Dot.

A Cat in a Box

Jim and Kim ran up to Dan.
Jim had a box.
"Look into the box," said Jim
to Dan.

"A fox!" said Dan.

"It's not a fox!" said Jim.

"It's Little Bud, a cat," said Kim.
"See him pop up."

"I have to fix the box for Bud,"
said Jim.
Jim and Kim hug Little Bud.

Mop the Van

Tom is Dan and Jan's dad.
He had a mop in his van.
"I have to mop the van," he said.
"It has lots of mud in it."

Tom mops and mops.
He sees a box in the van
and looks into it.
Little Bud hops up!

Little Bud has fun.
He can hop on the mop.

get	gets
let	lets
pet	pets
bet	bets
jet	jets
wet	wets
yet	

you

pat	got	lot	bat
pot	get	let	bit
pet	wet	jet	bet

Look at the Pets

Jan and Kim took little Pam
to look at pets.
Pam looks at cats and pups.

Pam ran to her dad.
"Can I get a pet?" she said.

Gus said, "You have a pup!"

"Can I get a cat?" said Pam.

"Not yet," said Gus.
"I cannot let you have a cat
and a pup."

Little Pam is sad.

Mud on a Pup

Gus got a tub for Pam's pup.
"Pam," he said, "you cannot let
your pup run in the mud.
Get your pup into the tub.
Get him wet and rub suds on him."

Pam gets her pup into the tub.
She wets him and rubs him.
"Is your pup wet yet?" said Gus.

"He is a wet pet," said Pam.

"He lets me get him wet," said Pam.
"He is not a bad pet."

A Big Jet

Sam took Jim and Jan
to look at jets.
"Can you see a jet?" said Sam.

"Not yet," said Jan.

"I can see a jet," said Jim.

"It's not a jet," said Jan.

"I bet it is," said Jim.

Sam looks up.
"It is a big jet," he said.

ten

men

pen   pens

hen   hens

Ben

dog   dogs

fog

hog   hogs

(looked)

pat	bit	tin	fig
pet	bet	ten	fog
pen	Ben	men	hog

Ten Hens and a Hog

Dad took Dan, Jan, and Tam
to see Ben.
Ben had a hog, a dog, and lots
of hens in big pens.
Tam and Dan ran to look
at the hens.

Jan looked at the hog.
Ben said, "A big hog has to have
a big pen."

Tam said, "A hen can fit in a
little pen."

"But I have ten hens," said Ben.
"I have to have a big pen
for ten hens."

A Big Fog

Ben had a big pigpen.
It had a fat hog, a big pig,
and ten little pigs in it.
He had a pen with ten hens in it.

"We can look at the pigs and hens,"
said Jan.
"We can see the hens dig for bugs."

Dan said, "We can see the hog in
the mud."
A big fog hid the sun.

"We cannot see the pigs
and the hens," said Tam.
"Fog is not fun."

Fix a Pen

Tam sat and looked at
Ben's pigpen.

Ben said, "I had to have the men
fix the pen.
Dogs dug at the pen.
The men had to fix it."

Tam said, "It's not fun to fix
a pigpen, is it?"

"If it's hot, it's not fun,"
said Ben.

bed   beds

led

fed

red

bad	lid	rid	bed
bud	led	red	red
bed			fed

A Little Red Hen

A little red hen is in Ben's pen.
Pam looked at the hen and said,
"Can I have the red hen
for a pet?"

Ben said, "If you can get a box
for it, you can have the red hen."

Pam ran and got a box
with a lid.
She fed the hen and led it
to the box.
The little red hen got into its
little red box.

A Pen for Little Red

Jim and Dan ran to see Pam's
little red hen.
Pam had a bed for her hen
in a box.

Dan said, "I cannot get your hen
to dip in her pan for a sip."

"The hen cannot hop in her box,"
said Jim.
"Little Red has to have a pen."

Pam sets Little Red in a pen.
The hen hops and hops.
She dips in her pan for a sip.

A Happy Hen

Gus said to Pam, "Have you fed your pets?"

"I fed the dog but not Little Red," she said.
"Little Red digs for bugs in her pen."

"Can she get lots of bugs?" said Gus.
"Lots," said Pam. "She is fed and happy."

beg	begs
leg	legs
peg	pegs

yes

good

wood

bag	pig	beg	yet
big	peg	peg	yes
beg		leg	

A Cut Leg

Jan ran into a peg of wood.
She cut her leg on it.
"Dad," she said, "I cannot run
and have fun with a cut leg."

"Yes, you can," said Dad.
"I can fix a pad for the cut
on your leg."

Jan sat on the bed,
and Dad fit a pad on her cut leg.

Jan said, "You are a good dad
to fix a cut leg."

"I am happy to fix it," he said.

Rags and the Peg

Rags has a peg of wood.
She runs with it and has
lots of fun.

Jan took the peg and hid it.
Rags looks and looks.
She can see it up on a box.

Rags gets up on her legs to get
the peg of wood.

"You got it!" said Jan.
"You are a good dog!"

Sit Up and Beg

"Sit up, Rags," said Dan.
"Sit up and beg!
Look, Mom!
Rags sits up and begs!"

"Yes, she can," said Mom.
"Good pup! Good Rags!
Run and get the peg of wood!"

Rags got the wood and took it
to Mom.

"Good dog!" said Mom.
Rags can beg and get pegs for Mom.

bell	bells
tell	tells
fell	
well	wells

(can't)

(my)

bed bell	fed fell	wet well	bell well tell

Dan's Leg

Dan fell and hit his leg.

He tells Jan,

"I fell and hit my leg.

I can't tell Dad.

He said I can't bat and run

if I am not well."

"You can tell Dad," said Jan.

"If you are not well, let Dad

look at your leg.

I bet he can fix it.

He had a pad for the cut on my leg.

Let's get him and tell him you fell."

Jan took Dan to tell Dad.

"Well, you fell and hit your leg,"
Dad said.

"I can tell it's red.

Let me look at it."

Dan sat on the bed,
and Dad looked at Dan's leg.

"My leg is not bad," said Dan.

"Tell me I can run and bat."

"Well," Dad tells Dan, "you can't
if you are not well.

But if you get well, you can bat
and run."

Bells for Cats

Sam got bells for Nat
and Little Bud.
He took Nat's bell to Jan.
"It's good for Nat to have a
bell," he tells her.

"My cat can have a tag and a
bell," said Jan.

Sam took Little Bud's bell to Jim.
"It's good for cats to have
bells and tags," Sam tells Jim.

"Well, Bud can have a tag
and a bell," said Jim.

bill	bills
fill	fills
hill	hills
pill	pills
sill	sills
will	
ill	

job

fell	bell	well	sill
fill	bill	will	hill
	sill	pill	will

A Big Bed for Rags

Rags can't fit into her little bed.
Jan got a big bed for Rags,
but Rags will not get into it.

"It's my job to get Rags
into her bed," said Jan.

Dan said, "Fill a pan with bits
of ham and set it in the bed.
Rags will get into the bed
to get the ham."

Jan fills a pan with ham
and sets it in the bed.
But Rags will not get into the bed.

"Mom and Dad will get a big bill
for the bed.
Mom and Dad will not be happy,"
said Jan.
Jan sets the ham on the sill.
Dan gets Rags.

"Rags," said Jan, "you can have
the ham on the sill if you
will sit in your bed."
She sets Rags in the bed
and pats her.

"Good Rags," said Dan,
"to sit in your big bed."
He gets the ham on the sill
for Rags.

On the Bus

Jim, Kim, and Pam are on the bus
with Gus, Pam's dad.
Gus runs the bus up a big hill.
The bus cannot get to the top of
the hill.
"The bus is in a rut,"
Gus tells Jim and Kim.
"It cannot run.
I will have to fix the bus.
It's my job to get it to run."

It's hot on the bus,
and Pam gets ill.
Jim ran to fill a cup for Pam.
Gus had a pill for her.
She got well.

pass

miss

kiss

hiss

mess

less

fuss

hit	miss	fun	pat
hiss	mess	fuss	pass
kiss	less		

Nat, Rags, and Bud

Nat ran to see Rags.
He has to pass Bud to get to Rags.
Will Bud hiss at Nat?

Bud did not hiss
but ran with Nat to see Rags.
Rags can see the cats have fun.
She will run with Nat and Bud.
Nat, Bud, and Rags hop up
on Jan's bed.

Jan runs in and sees the mess.
"My bed is a mess!" she said.
"Bad Nat! Bad Bud! Bad Rags!
It's bad to mess up my bed."

I Miss Bud

"I miss Bud," said Jim to Kim.
"Is he with you?"

"He is not with me," Kim tells Jim.
"Is he with Tam and her pup?"

Jim and Kim run to see Tam.
"Is Bud with your pup?" said Kim.

"I can't fuss with dogs and cats,"
said Tam.
"I have to cook ham for Mom
and Dad."

Jim and Kim run to see Jan.
Jan said, "My bed is a mess."

"Did Bud mess up your bed?"
said Jim.

"Bud, Nat, and Rags did it,"
said Jan.
Jim and Kim took Bud and set
him in his bed.

Jan can fix her bed.
It is less of a mess.

"I had a kiss for Bud," said Kim.
"But he is a bad cat!"

back	backs
jack	jacks
pack	packs
sack	sacks

went

sat	bat	pat	pack
sack	back	pack	sack
			jack

A Sack of Jacks

"Dad got me a big sack of jacks,"
said Pam to Dan.

"My mom got me a pack
for my back," said Dan.
"Let's run and see Tam with
my pack and your jacks."

Tam's mom said, "Tam and her dad
went into the woods to get logs.
Tam taps the backs of logs to get
rid of bugs.
Her dad fits the logs into sacks.
Sit on your pack.
She will be back."

A Backpack for Tam

Tam went to her mom.
"Is Dad in the den?" she said.

"Yes," said Tam's mom, "he is
in the den."

Tam went to see her dad.
"Pam got a sack of jacks.
And Dan got a pack for his back,"
Tam said to her dad.

Dad said, "Well, I got a backpack
for you!
You can pack it with lots of jacks!"

Tam went to fill her backpack.
She filled it with packs of gum,
her sack of jacks, and a pot
and a pan.
She took it to Jim and Kim.

"I got a backpack," she said.
"I can have it on my back."

"Let's backpack in the woods,"
said Jim.
"We can cook a bit
and have fun in the woods."

neck	necks
deck	decks
peck	pecks

pack	peck	neck	pecks
peck	neck	deck	necks
			decks

Rags and the Hens

Dad is on the sun deck. Rags runs into the pen with Ben's hens. A big fat hen pecks at her. Rags yips and runs back to Dad on the sun deck.

Dad pats Rags on the back, and Rags rubs her neck on Dad's leg. "Be good, Rags," Dad tells her. "Sit with me, and Ben's hens will not peck at you."

On the Sun Deck

Pam took Little Red up on the sun deck. "We can sit in the sun and have lots of fun," she said.

Little Red pecks for bugs on the deck. The hen pecks and pecks.

"It's good for Little Red to peck for bugs," said Pam. "The sun deck is good for her."

The Men Fix a Deck

"It's a job to fix the sun deck," said Dad.

"Yes," said Gus. "Cut wood gets on necks and on backs."

Gus tells Pam, "Pass my kit. I have to hit a peg into the wood." Gus taps the peg into the deck.

"It's a mess," said Pam. "Bits of wood hit my neck."

At six Dad and Gus did fix the deck. Pam looked happy.

"Decks are bad to fix," she said, "but good to sit on."

sick

Nick

pick   picks

lick   licks

Doctor

spot

peck	neck	sack	sick
pack	Nick	sick	pick
pick			lick

Kim Is Sick

Kim is sick. She has a big red spot on her neck. She has a red spot on her leg. Her dad got Doctor Nick to look at her.

The doctor tells Kim's dad, "Kim will have to be in bed, and you will have to pick up pills for her."

Kim took a pill at six and at ten. She will not be sick. She will not have red spots.

Up and Well

It's six, and Kim is up. She runs to her dad and mom. "I took my pills and I am well," she said.

"The red spots are not on her legs and neck," Dad tells Mom.

Dad picks Kim up and sets her on the bed. Mom hugs Kim.

"It's bad to be sick," said Kim. "But it's good to get well."

Bud Is Sick

"Little Bud looks sick," said Jim. He picks Bud up and sets him in his bed.

Jim sets Bud's pan in his bed. But Bud will not lick at it. Jim tells Kim, "Bud is sick."

Kim said, "Set a pan of ham in Bud's bed. If he is sick, he will not lick at the ham."

Jim sets the ham in Bud's bed. Bud licks at it.

"Bud took the ham," said Kim. "He is not sick."

rock	rocks
lock	locks
sock	socks

very

lick lock	sick sock	lock rock	socks rocks locks

A Bad Cut

Little Pam and her pup ran up a hill. Pam fell and cut her leg on a big rock. Her pup ran to get Gus.

Gus picked Pam up. He looked at the cut and said, "It's not a very big cut."

Gus had pads for cuts in his little kit, but the kit had a lock on it. "My kit is locked," said Gus. "I can't get at the pads. Locks can be bad."

Gus picked at the lock. He hit it. Pop went the lock!

Pam sat, and Gus fixed the cut. "It's good to run," he said. "But look for big rocks."

"I will," said Pam. She had a hug and a kiss for Gus.

Pam's Socks

Dan sat on the rocks with Pam. He looked at her socks and said, "Pam, you have a tan sock and a red sock."

"It's not a tan sock," Pam said. "It's mud on my red sock. I ran and fell in the mud. I have mud on my legs and on my sock."

Dan said, "Well, a little suds will fix your legs and your socks."

duck   ducks

luck

tuck   tucks

story

lick	luck	deck	ducks
lock	tuck	duck	tucks
luck			

The Duck and the Fox

Gus tucks Pam into bed and tells her a story. It's the story of a big fox and a little duck.

A little duck went into the woods. A big red fox had its den in the woods. The fox looked for the duck, but the duck hid in a little log.

"I am in luck!" said the duck. "A big fox can't get into a little log."

"Bad luck!" said the fox. "I can't get at the little duck."

Little Duck and the Bug

"The story of the duck and the fox is a good story," Pam said. "Tuck me in and tell me the story of Little Duck and the bug."

Gus tells Pam the story.

A bug sits on a log in the woods. Little Duck pecks at the bug. But the bug hops on Little Duck's neck and nips it.

"I can't sit on a log and have fun if you peck at me," said the bug to Little Duck.

Little Duck said, "Bugs are happy on logs."

"Yes," said the bug, "but not if you peck me."

"I will not peck at you," said Little Duck, "if you will not nip at my neck."

"Ducks are not bad," said the bug. "I will not nip at your neck."

"I am happy you will not nip me," said Little Duck. "Good luck to you."

that

than

them

then

this

cat mat that	man can than	pen men then	then them this

This and That

Gus had packs of nuts for Jan and for Pam. "This pack of nuts is for Jan," he said. "It is big. That pack is for Pam. Pam is little and gets less than Jan."

Jan said, "I have lots of nuts. I will let Jim, Kim, and Dan have a bit."

Jan ran to them with the nuts. Then the kids said, "Very good nuts!"

Books for Jan and Dan

Mom tells Jan and Dan to look in her big sack. In the sack are books for them.

"This is a good book for you, Jan," said Mom. "It's the story of a fox and her good luck."

Then Dan said, "Is that book for me?"

"Yes," said Mom, "that is your book. It's a big book of cats and dogs."

Jan and Dan took the books. Dan sat in the sun and looked at his book.

Kim ran up. "That looks as if it's a good book," she said to Dan.

"It is," said Dan. Then he said, "Jan got a good book. It's the story of a fox. This book is the story of lots of dogs and cats."

thin

thick

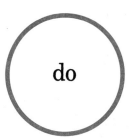

do

Nick sick thick	pin win thin	thick thin	thin thick

The Sick Cat

Kim said to Jim, "Bud looks thin and sad. We have to get Doctor Bell to look at him."

Doctor Bell looked at Bud and said, "That cat is thin. Do you have catnip for him?"

"We do," said Jim.

Doctor Bell said, "Let Bud have a thick bit of catnip. He will not be sad. Then you can cut bits of ham for him to lick."

Jim and Kim took Bud and set him on a thick mat. "Do you have that catnip?" said Kim.

"Yes, I do," said Jim.

He set the catnip on the mat. He set the ham on the mat. Bud is happy to have the catnip. He licked the ham. Then Bud got well. He did not look thin and sad. He looked happy.

Dad's Story

Pam and Dan beg Dan's dad to tell them a story.

"This is the story of a big dog," said Dad. "He looks as if he has thick socks on his legs."

Dad went on. "This dog runs into a thick woods. He sees a thin fox. With his leg, the dog pats the fox. The fox nips, and the dog runs."

Dad tells them, "But the leg is not cut. The dog is happy he can run."

bath   baths

path   paths

math

(by)

bag	pan	map	path
bath	path	math	bath
			math

A Bath for Rags

Dad and Rags went on a path into the woods. A little fox ran by. Rags ran to look at it.

"Get back on the path, Rags!" said Dad.

Rags got back on the path, but she had lots of mud on her. She had to have a bath.

Dad got Rags into the tub. He had to rub her with thick, hot suds. The mud and suds got on Dad. Then Dad had to have a bath!

Dan's Math

"I have to do this math if I am to pass," Dan said.

"You will do well," said Mom. "Can you do it by six?"

"Yes," said Dan. He looked at the math book.

"I can't do this math," he said. He is not happy.

He took the math book to his mom. She sat by him, and he did his math well.

"That's good!" said Mom. "See? You can do it!"

Fun for Tam and Kim

Tam kicks a little rock on a path. "This is fun," she tells Kim. "Do it with me."

"I have to be back by six to do math and get a bath," said Kim.

"I have to be back then to look at my books and get my bath," said Tam.

Kim and Tam kick rocks up the paths. Tam runs to kick them back.

Kim and Tam have to run to be back for baths by six.

chin	chins
chip	chips
chick	chicks
check	checks
chop	chops

much

such

tin	top	Nick	deck
pin	pop	lick	neck
chin	chop	chick	check

Ben's Chicks

Ben's hens had ten little chicks. The chicks peck for bugs. The hens check to see that the chicks are fed.

Ben checks them in the pen. The pen has a bad spot. Ben chops wood to fix the spot. Chop, chop!

Wood chips get on a chick. Ben picks the chick up. The little chick is well. Ben sets it back in the pen by a hen. The chick looks up and runs to Ben.

"I can't get much fixed with this chick," said Ben.

Bits and Chips

The kids looked at Ben's chicks. Jan had bits of buns and chips in a sack. She set a chip in the pen. A chick pecked at it.

"Look, the chick missed," said Dan. "Let it have lots." Jan took lots of bits for the chick. The chick pecked and got a bit of bun.

"Chicks do not have chins," said Jan. "For a chin, a chick has a bill."

Dan said, "Such bits and chips can fit in a little bill. A big bun can't fit."

Mom's Checks

"I have to have the checks," said Mom. "I have to look at them and fix the checkbook."

Mom looks at the checks and at the checkbook. "We have missed a check," she said. "It's not for much, but I have to look for it."

She looks and looks. She sees the check in the back of a book.

Grandma

Grandpa

no
so
go

| no so | no go | so no go | go so no |

At Grandma and Grandpa's

Dan and Jan went to Grandma's on the bus. Nat went with them. Grandma and Grandpa met them at the bus.

"You are so big!" said Grandma as she picked up Jan and Dan's bag.

"Let's go!" said Grandpa. "We have so much to do!"

"We will have such fun at Grandma and Grandpa's," said Jan.

Jan's Bath

Grandma said to Jan, "Go get a bath in my big bathtub. I will go and fill Nat's pan. He will be fed and you can go to bed."

Grandma went to look for Nat. She said to Grandpa, "Did Nat go by you?"

"No," said Grandpa. "Look for Jan. I bet Nat is with Jan."

Grandma looked in. Nat sat by the tub. "Nat will not get in with me," said Jan.

"Good," said Grandma.

Jan, Dan, and Grandpa

Jan, Dan, and Grandpa went into the woods. Grandpa took a bag of chips, and the kids took sacks of nuts.

A thick fog fell and hid the path. "We will have to sit on that log for a bit. Then the fog will go, and we can see the path," said Grandpa.

Jan, Dan, and Grandpa sat on the log and had chips and nuts.

"This is fun," said Jan.

"It is a bit of luck that we had fog," said Dan.

catch

patch

match

latch

ranch

bench

horse   was

| mat match latch | pat patch catch | ran ranch | Ben bench |

The Big Red Horse

Grandpa tucked Dan into bed, and Dan said, "Will you tell me a story, Grandpa?"

"Yes, Dan, I will tell you a good story," said Grandpa.

The cat took a nap on a bench. The pigs ran in a patch of mud and had fun. But Big Red, the horse, was sad.

Big Red said good-by to the cat on the bench and the pigs in the mud. He ran into the woods. He can run and have fun in the woods. He will not go back to the ranch. Big Red was happy.

Then a man yelled. It was Jud. He was mad. "I can catch horses," he said. "I will catch Big Red, and he will go back to my ranch. He will buck and kick, but I will lock him in a horse pen with a big latch on it. He will not run in the woods!"

But Big Red did run. He ran and ran. He ran on rocks and in mud. He ran to the hills and hid.

Jud was no match for Big Red. He did not catch the horse.

The big red horse will miss the woods. He will miss the cat and the pigs, but he will not miss the horse pen with the big latch. He will run in the hills, and he will be happy.

inch

pinch

punch

lunch

bunch

sky

bun	bunch	pin	in
bunch	lunch	pinch	inch
	punch		

Grandma's Story

Jan and Dan cooked lunch for Grandma and Grandpa. Jan cut ham an inch thick. Then she mixed a punch. "I will fix hot buns with a pinch of this and a pinch of that," Dan said. "Then Grandma will tell us a story."

This is Grandma's story.

Little Red Hen was in the woods. A nut fell and hit her. "The sky fell on me!" she yelled. "I will go tell the duck." So Little Red Hen ran to tell the duck.

"My, my, that's bad!" said the duck. "Let's go tell the fat pig." So the hen and the duck ran to tell the pig.

"My, my," said the pig, "that's bad! Let's go tell the horse." So the hen, the duck, and the pig ran to tell the horse.

"My, my, that's bad!" said the horse to the hen. "Let's go tell the fox."

The duck pecked at the latch on the horse's pen. The hen, the duck, and the pig got up on the horse's back. Then the bunch went into the woods to look for the fox.

"The sky fell on me!" said the hen to the fox.

The fox looked at the sky. Then she looked at the path. "No, it was not the sky that fell," said the fox. "Look, it's a little nut. A nut fell on you, Red Hen."

itch

pitch

Dr.

| patch | pitch | pitch | itch |
| pitch | itch | pinch | inch |

Pills for a Horse

The sun had set, but it was hot. Dan said, "I am hot, and my legs itch."

Grandma said, "Go in and have a bath. You will not be so hot. Then you can look at TV with us."

This was the story on TV.

Dr. Mack was a horse doctor. She went to Good Luck Ranch to look at Ken and Pat's sick horse.

"Dr. Mack," Pat said, "Jet kicked and bucked. He pitched us into the mud. Jet is very sick. He got a chill. We cannot let a horse pitch us. He has to get well."

"Do not look so sad," Dr. Mack said to her. "It will not be much of a job to get Jet well. I have horse pills for sick horses."

It was a big pill. But it was not much for a big horse. Jet took it.

Jet got well. He ran and kicked. Pat and Ken are happy Jet is well. Jet is happy Dr. Mack had big horse pills.

TO THE TEACHER

The MERRILL READING PROGRAM consists of eight Readers developed on linguistic principles applicable to the teaching of reading. The rationale of the program and detailed teaching procedures are described in the Teacher's Edition of each Reader.

All words introduced in this Reader are listed on the following pages under the headings "Words in Pattern," "Sight Words," and "Applications of Patterning."

Words listed as "Words in Pattern" represent additional matrices in the first major set of spelling patterns. The vowel letters o and e are introduced in the matrices of this Reader. New consonant-letter combinations in the matrices of this Reader are *ll, ss, ck, th, ch, tch,* and *nch.* This Reader also introduces *y, th,* and *ch* in initial positions.

Words listed as "Sight Words" are high-frequency words introduced to provide normal sentence patterns in the stories.

Words listed as "Applications of Patterning" include new words based on patterns and sight words previously introduced, combinations of words (compound words), additional tense forms, plurals, and possessives.

WORD LISTS FOR TEACHER REFERENCE

Pages	Words in Pattern		Sight Words
Unit 1 5-8	pot cot lot Dot hot	pots cots lots dots	
	mom		
Unit 2 9-12	hop mop pop top	hops mops pops tops	
	box fox		
Unit 3 13-16	get let pet bet jet wet yet	gets lets pets bets jets wets	you
Unit 4 17-20	ten men pen hen Ben	pens hens	looked
	dog fog hog	dogs hogs	
Unit 5 21-24	bed led fed red	beds	

Pages	Words in Pattern		Sight Words
Unit 6 25-28	beg leg peg yes	begs legs pegs	good wood
Unit 7 29-32	bell tell fell well	bells tells wells	can't my
Unit 8 33-36	bill fill hill pill sill will ill job	bills fills hills pills sills	
Unit 9 37-40	pass miss kiss hiss mess less fuss		
Unit 10 41-44	back jack pack sack	backs jacks packs sacks	went
Unit 11 45-48	neck deck peck	necks decks pecks	

Pages	Words in Pattern	Sight Words
Unit 12 49-52	sick Nick pick picks lick licks	Doctor spot
Unit 13 53-56	rock rocks lock locks sock socks	very
Unit 14 57-60	duck ducks luck tuck tucks	story
Unit 15 61-64	that than them then this	
Unit 16 65-68	thin thick	do
Unit 17 69-72	bath baths path paths math	by
Unit 18 73-76	chin chins chip chips chick chicks check checks chop chops much such	

Pages	Words in Pattern	Sight Words
Unit 19 77-80		Grandma Grandpa no so go
Unit 20 81-84	catch patch match latch ranch bench	horse was
Unit 21 85-88	inch pinch punch lunch bunch	sky
Unit 22 89-91	itch pitch	Dr.

Applications of Patterning
(The underlined numbers are page numbers.)

Unit 1 5-8 cook Dot's	Unit 8 33-36 be rut set	Unit 14 57-60 Duck's log nip nips	Unit 19 77-80 bathtub Grandma's Grandpa's met
Unit 2 9-12 hip Tom	Unit 9 37-40	Unit 15 61-64 book books kids	Unit 20 81-84 buck good-by horses Jud tucked yelled
Unit 3 13-16 cats	Unit 10 41-44 backpack den filled logs we woods	Unit 16 65-68 catnip licked	
Unit 4 17-20 Ben's dug pigpen			Unit 21 85-88 an cooked horse's mixed
Unit 5 21-24 its sets sip	Unit 11 45-48 yips	Unit 17 69-72 kick kicks that's	
	Unit 12 49-52 spots		Unit 22 89-91 bucked chill Ken kicked Mack Pat's pitched TV
Unit 6 25-28	Unit 13 53-56 fixed locked pads picked	Unit 18 73-76 checkbook missed Mom's pecked	
Unit 7 29-32 Bud's let's			